TIME FOR KIDS READERS

Sun Power

by Susan Ring

Harcourt

Orlando   Austin   Chicago   New York   Toronto   London   San Diego

Visit The Learning Site!
www.harcourtschool.com

The sun is hot and bright. It warms
the water, the land, and people, too.

Plants use sunlight to make their own food. People have learned how to use sunlight, too.

The roof on this house has special panels that hold in sunlight. Sun power can be used to warm the house. The sun power will also be used to make electricity and turn on the lights.

One day, you may drive a solar car.

Some cars don't need any gas. They use sun power to make the car go. Cars like this help keep the air clean

Solar panels

5

This is a sun power plant. It makes power for many people.

The mirrors move to follow the sun all day long.

This solar watch is one tool that uses sun power. Tiny parts inside hold the light.

Sun power makes things go—even on Mars.

<u>Sojourner</u>, a
robot vehicle,
explored Mars.